Introduction

Even if you are just getting started, practising mindfulness meditation can have many positive effects on your mind and body. These include reduced anxiety, obsessive, repetitive thoughts and muscle tension, and increased focus, clarity and productivity.

Some studies even show that mindfulness meditation can physically change your brain by increasing the thickness of the areas associated with memory, empathy, and stress regulation.

Learning mindfulness meditation with guidance from a trained and qualified teacher will help you understand the benefits and how it works and techniques to gain the most from it. At Meditation Sunshine Coast, I teach mindfulness meditation using attention regulation techniques, such as focussing on your breathing, senses and body sensations, to train your mind to be present.

A present mind cultivates a calm mind.

With this simple but comprehensive guide, I will help you on your journey to cultivating a calm mind, by integrating mindfulness and meditation into your daily life.

Dislcaimer: The information, exercises and meditations in this book are intended for general interest and use and not as therapy or treatment for any mental or physical condition. Please seek the advice and services of a professional health practitioner for the treatment of any disorder or if you are at all concerned about your physical, mental or emotional wellbeing.

Table of Contents

1. Mindfulness

6	What is Mindfulness?
7	Mindfulness Tips for Everyday Life
11	Mindfulness Questionnaire
13	Daily Mindfulness Record

2. Meditation

15	What is Meditation?
17	The Benefits
19	How it Works
20	The Stress Response
21	Meditation Questionnaire

3. Getting Started

24	Tips To Get Started
25	Steps to Get Started
27	Common Obstacles
30	Setting Up Your Practice

4. Breathing Techniques

32	Breathing Insights
33	Anchor Points
34	Breathing Exercises

- Belly Breathing
- Counting the Breath
- Box Breathing

5. Body Relaxation

39   About Muscles

41   The Relaxation Response

42   Relaxation Exercises

- PMR
- Body Scan
- Pain Release

6. Managing Thoughts

49   The Thinking Mind

50   Bringing Awareness to Your Thoughts

51   Techniques for Managing Thoughts

53   Contemplation Exercises

- Thought Cloud Exercise
- Thought Train Exercise
- Starfish Meditation

7. Releasing Emotions

57   The Science of Emotions

58   Emotions in the Body

59   Working with Emotions

61   Releasing Exercises

- Colour Breath
- Mantras and Mudras
- R.A.I.N.

8. What Next

66   28 Day Meditation Plan

69   Continue Your Journey

9. About Me

1. MINDFULNESS

> "Mindfulness is about being aware of the present moment and ourselves. By focussing on the here and now, and suspending the judgement of our thoughts, feelings and experience, we are able to cultivate a sense of peace, clarity and acceptance."
>
> Michelle Eckles

WHAT IS MINDFULNESS?

Simply put, mindfulness is a way of paying attention. It's a practice that helps us focus on what we're sensing and feeling in each moment - so we don't lose sight of what's happening around us.

More often than not, we're running on autopilot or distracted by our thoughts and feelings, rather than being present. We may not even notice when we have drifted off and lost minutes or even hours. Practising mindfulness brings us back into our bodies and ourselves - the only place where genuine, long-lasting happiness resides.

In more detail, mindfulness is about:

- Being present and paying attention to our surroundings - detaching from past and future thoughts reduces obsessive worrying and overthinking, which can cause anxiety and depression.

- Observing our senses, thoughts, and emotions without judgment - this can help cultivate peace and acceptance and reduce negative thought patterns, as you aren't looking for what's wrong with any given moment.

- Developing self-awareness - being more aware of our thoughts, feelings, and emotions and how we respond to them can help us make better choices.

- Becoming more compassionate, and empathetic to ourselves and those around us - creating kind communities.

Mindfulness is innate - we were born with the ability to practice it.

If leading a high-paced life on autopilot means you have lost the natural ability to be mindful, don't despair. You can still cultivate it!

It simply means living your life deliberately, and consciously attending to what's happening around you and inside you at any given moment. While meditation is a way you can practise mindfulness, there are countless other opportunities, like on your morning work or eating your evening meal.

The key is simply bringing awareness to your thoughts and actions, as well as non-judgemental curiosity, no matter what they may be.

MINDFULNESS TIPS

 ## DRIVING

How often have you driven from A to B and not remembered how you got there? Or driven to the wrong place, like to school on the school holidays (I've done that before!).

Here are some mindfulness tips for driving:

- When you sit in the driver seat, notice how comfortable you are, including things like your posture.

- Notice the feeling of the steering wheel in your hands and your feet on the pedals.

- Repeat in your mind where you are going, e.g. I am driving to the shops.

- As you drive, notice where you are looking – mirrors, the road, colours of the other cars.

- Put your phone on "do not disturb" whilst you are driving.

- Practise "belly breathing" when you are stopped at lights – feeling your tummy inflate on the in-breath and deflate on the out-breath.

- Is there anything in your car that doesn't need to be there, e.g. rubbish, clothing, empty water bottles, old street directories, expired rego certificates.

 ## EATING

How often have you eaten a meal without tasting the food? Perhaps you forgot what you had for breakfast?

Here are some mindfulness tips for eating:

- At your next family meal, make everyone change positions from their usual seat at the table – you will be surprised at how much more alert you feel!

- Before you dish up, ask yourself how hungry you are on a scale of 1-10, then listen to your body.

- Slow your eating down and chew each mouthful for a count of 10.

- Stop eating as soon as you begin to feel full – if you burp, you have eaten enough.

- Before you eat your next item of food, pause, pay attention to and consider its:
    - Shape
    - Size
    - Weight
    - Texture
    - Temperature
    - Smell
    - Taste as you take your first bite
    - Source of origin
    - Method of growing or production

EXERCISING

If you are anything like me, exercising is something I want to get over and done with to feel the after effect.

Physical activity is good for releasing the stress hormone cortisol, so it is beneficial for mental wellbeing, not just physical.

Here are some tips to exercising mindfully, so that you get the most out of it:

- Set your intention when you begin exercising as to what aspect you are going to practise being mindful about, e.g.:

    - Swimming - you could focus on the feel of the water.

    - Cycling - you could focus on your grip on the handlebars.

    - Running - you could focus on the feel of the surface beneath your feet.

    - Walking - you could focus on the colours around you.

- Coordinate your breath with your movement, e.g. when doing push-ups, breathe in as you lower your body and breathe out as you push up.

- To bring your heart rate down, breathe in and out through your nostrils. This is also a more efficient way of breathing than through your mouth, which tends to be quick and shallow instead of slow and long.

- When rehydrating, drink slowly and intentionally.

- When finished, lay quietly and notice what sensations you are feeling.

 # HOUSEWORK

In a self-care workshop I run, participants are often surprised that some feel emotional or mental wellbeing after finishing household chores. Just like physical exercise, there are additional benefits to performing household chores such as:

- Clearing clutter = helps clear mental clutter.

- Having a clean workspace = can help you be more productive.

- Filing or doing your budget or tax return = relieves stress and anxiety.

- Cooking a nice meal = tells your body you love it.

Here are some mindfulness tips for performing household chores to make them more enjoyable, hopefully!

- Vacuuming – notice the sounds of the vacuum cleaner.

- Dishes – notice the temperature of the water on your hands.

- Making your bed – notice the colours or patterns in your blanket or duvet cover.

- Feeding pets – notice the gratitude with which they receive their food.

- Cooking – notice the individual texture and smells of the things you cut and cook.

- Washing – peg each item slowly and methodically, counting how many you use.

WORKING

We spend so much of our time at work, and work-related stress is at an all-time high.

Here are some mindfulness tips for making your workday less stressful and more productive:

- Start your day by writing a to-do list - keep it achievable and focus only on the things that need to be done that day.

- Stop trying to multitask - close all those tabs and focus on one thing at a time. You will be so much more efficient and productive.

- Don't eat at your desk on autopilot whilst doing other things - take your lunch outside and eat it mindfully.

- Schedule regular breaks - get up and stretch.

- Observe your colleagues - connect with someone to see how they are feeling.

- Get yourself a plant - bring some nature into your office (plus natural sunlight if possible).

- Clean your workspace at the end of the day - you will start your next day clear and refreshed.

- Turn off your notifications - they interrupt your flow.

- Don't take devices to meetings - bring your full attention.

- Listen during conversations - to clients, colleagues, suppliers.

MINDFULNESS QUESTIONNAIRE

The Mindful Attention Awareness Scale (MAAS)

The MAAS assesses a core characteristic of mindfulness - a receptive state of mind that is aware of what's occurring in the present and observing what is happening.

Below is a collection of statements about your everyday experience. Using the 1-6 scale below, please indicate how frequently or infrequently you have each experience in the right-hand column. Please answer according to what reflects your experience rather than what you think your experience should be. Please treat each question separately from every other one.

To score, calculate the average of the 15 items (add the scores together, then divide by 15). The higher the score, the higher the level of mindfulness. Repeat this questionnaire after practising mindfulness meditation for 28 days to compare the difference.

1	2	3	4	5	6
almost always	very frequently	somewhat frequently	somewhat infrequently	very infrequently	almost never

1. I could be experiencing some emotion and not be conscious of it until sometime later.

2. I break or spill things because of carelessness, not paying attention, or thinking of something else.

3. I find it difficult to stay focussed on what's happening in the present.

4. I tend to walk quickly to get where I'm going without paying attention to what I experience along the way.

5. I tend not to notice feelings of physical tension or discomfort until they really grab my attention.

6. I forget a person's name almost as soon as I've been told it for the first time.

7. It seems I am "running on automatic," without much awareness of what I'm doing.

8. I rush through activities without being really attentive to them.

9. I get so focussed on the goal I want to achieve that I lose touch with what I'm doing right now to get there.

10. I do jobs or tasks automatically, without being aware of what I'm doing.

11. I find myself listening to someone with one ear, doing something else at the same time.

12. I drive places on 'automatic pilot' and then wonder why I went there.

13. I find myself preoccupied with the future or the past.

14. I find myself doing things without paying attention.

15. I snack without being aware that I'm eating.

YOUR SCORE NOW:

YOUR SCORE AFTER PRACTISING MINDFULNESS FOR 28 DAYS:

Brown, K.W. & Ryan, R.M. (2003). The benefits of being present: Mindfulness and its role in psychological well-being. *Journal of Personality and Social Psychology, 84*, 822-848.

DAILY MINDFULNESS RECORD

Over the next seven days, choose an activity to practice mindfully. Record what activity you did, what your focus or mindful intention was, and how you felt or what sensations you noticed afterwards.

Try to do at least one activity from the tips in this chapter, with mindful intention each day, even if it's just getting dressed or brushing your teeth.

Day	Activity	Focus or Intention	What you noticed

2. MEDITATION

> "Meditation practice isn't about trying to throw ourselves away and become something better, it's about befriending who we are."
>
> Ani Pema Chodron

WHAT IS MEDITATION?

For thousands of years, monks in Eastern countries have been practising meditation. In more recent times, mindfulness has grown in popularity in the West. Here is a brief history of meditation:

Originating in China and India, monks were the first to practise meditation.

In the 1950s, large-scale immigration from Asia to America, due to the communist invasion in China, brought Asian teachers to the West, strengthing and widening their audience.

During the psychedelic revolution of the 1960s, people used it to reach a state of higher consciousness.

The health and lifestyle benefits of meditation became evident in the 1970s. Over time various studies showed its effectiveness in treating a wide range of physical, mental, and emotional stressors.

Mindfulness Meditation is:

- A formal way to practise mindfulness.
- A method for achieving mental clarity and emotional calm.
- A mental discipline requiring focussed awareness.
- A technique that uses attention regulation of the breath, senses or body sensations to train our minds to be present.
- Secular, practical, and easy to learn with many physical, mental, and emotional benefits.

> You don't need to practise meditation to be mindful, but you do need to practise mindfulness to meditate.

Meditation techniques are like modes of transport – there are different ways to arrive at the same destination, e.g. boat, plane, train, car. There are many methods, techniques and styles of meditation. Some of them are specific to a spiritual or cultural tradition, time period, text, teacher, or personal philosophy, e.g. Vipassana meditation is from Theravada Buddhism, and Transcendental Meditation is from Vedantic Hinduism.

Examples of other meditation techniques:

- RELAXATION
  Yoga Nidra

- SOUND
  music, chanting, singing bowls

- MANTRA
  affirmations, mala beads, transcendental

- MOVING
  Tai Chi, Chi Gong, walking, labyrinths, dancing, yoga

- ART
  drawing, mandalas

- INSIGHT
  finding a solution to a problem or answer to a question

THE BENEFITS OF MINDFULNESS MEDITATION

The most well-known, publicised and researched benefit for meditating is stress reduction. Meditation research has shown that it can lower blood pressure, boost immunity, and relieve depression and anxiety. These are just some of the many reasons people choose to meditate.

Maybe you're looking for a way to cope with illness or injury or want to get in better touch with your inner self.

Whatever your reasoning, there's no denying that mindfulness meditation is a tool that can help achieve this and more!

Learning to meditate can seem challenging, but it can make everyday life much easier. Here are some practical reasons why it's worth trying.

In everyday life, meditation can help you to:

- Relax physically and mentally.
- Relieve stress and tension.
- Promote peaceful and harmonious relationships.
- Increase productivity at work and home.
- Improve performance in sport.
- Enhance focus and concentration.
- Cultivate self-confidence.
- Develop self-awareness and self-control.
- Identify unhealthy thinking patterns and replace them with more positive ones.
- Connect with intuition and insight.

 ## PHYSICAL BENEFITS

As you become more aware of your internal and external body sensations:

- Decreases restlessness - as you learn it's okay to be still and do nothing.

- Releases muscle tension, body aches, and pain - as you begin to tune into your body's needs and what it's trying to tell you. A body that's constantly on high alert is a recipe for stress and chronic disease.

- Helps the body relax and sleep - as you learn to switch off the mind chatter.

- Develops the ability to tune into your senses - providing greater enjoyment of day-to-day experiences.

- Increases productivity at school, work, and sport - as your body feels rested and refreshed.

 ## EMOTIONAL BENEFITS

As you become more aware of your feelings and reactions to them:

- Enables the ability to feel and process emotions without being overwhelmed by them - as you practice allowing and accepting rather than avoiding.

- Builds self-esteem and resilience - as you learn to accept and not judge your thoughts and feelings.

- Improves the ability to react in a more thoughtful, calm, and less reactive way in challenging situations - as you learn to pause and engage other parts of your brain.

- Builds peaceful and harmonious relationships with friends and family - learning about your own emotions creates empathy for others.

 ## MENTAL BENEFITS

As you become more aware of distracting thoughts and things that stress you:

- Quiets the mind chatter and excessive thinking by staying present and not thinking about the past or the future.

- Relieves stress and increases the ability to cope with stressful situations - as you get to know yourself and begin to build your inner strengths and resources.

- Enhances focus and concentration - as you learn to regulate your attention.

HOW MINDFULNESS MEDITATION WORKS

Mindfulness meditation uses an anchor point to keep your attention focussed.

When you focus on something like the sensation of the breath and following each inhalation and exhalation, you become less distracted by thoughts. You can relax your mind and enjoy the present moment and all it offers.

It's a great way to develop self-awareness by learning to remain calm and peaceful even when your mind is racing with thoughts about what you have to do tomorrow, or something stressful that happened yesterday.

Practising meditation:

- Brings the body back into a state of homeostasis - enabling it to rest, recover and perform optimally.

- Gives a busy or distracted mind something else to do - reducing anxiety and depression and increasing focus and clarity.

- Weakens the brain's stress signal - enabling a more thoughtful response to challenging or stressful situations.

- Increases the quality of our attention - paying attention lights up the brain, turbocharging the neurons in the prefrontal cortex.

- Aids in cognitive functions such as memory and learning - by sustaining states of stillness for prolonged periods.

Practising mindfulness also creates a mental space or pause between impulse and action. This enables us to replace unconscious and rushed habits or reactions with more conscious and thoughtful responses and reactions.

Growing research also shows that practising meditation long term can preserve our telomeres, which are the protective caps on the end of our chromosomes. These usually shorten with age and illnesses like heart disease and Alzheimer's.

THE STRESS RESPONSE

When we get stressed or fearful, several things happen in our brains:

- The Amygdala is activated - the emotional response centre.

- The Prefrontal Cortex is deactivated - the logical, decision making, problem-solving intelligence centre.

- The Amygdala coordinates a response to the threat - by sending the flow of blood to areas like our arms and legs so they can run away, defend us or hide, aka Fight, Flight or Freeze.

There are three stages to the stress cycle:

 **Reaction or Response** (fight, flight or freeze)

 **Safety** (the threat is over)

 **Recovery** (body goes back into homeostasis)

In the event of something threatening your life, e.g. a shark attack, you want your body to go through those three stages.

Stressful events can cause us to go into stage one, but in the absence of an actual physical threat to use the excess energy (and stress hormone cortisol) when we go into fight or flight, the body can stay in this stress response.

Staying in this response mode for prolonged periods and not going through the safety and recovery modes can cause wear and tear on the body and impaired mental performance.

The bad news is that we can get into this same level of stress as a shark attack might induce, without noticing it, just by being busy with our everyday lives or being stuck in traffic or having an argument with your partner or boss. The good news is that practising meditation can shrink the Amygdala and weaken its connection.

Practising mindfulness and meditation enables us to recognise and neutralise the fight or flight response mode, and react with a more thoughtful response to stress via other parts of the brain (by engaging the Prefrontal Cortex).

MEDITATION QUESTIONNAIRE

People practise meditation for many different reasons or may even start with one reason that changes over time. I began meditating to stop feeling so overwhelmed, then I used it for creative thinking, and now I use it mainly to start my day calm and composed.

This tool is to assist with identifying your reasons for wanting to learn meditation and the benefits that may be of relevance or interest to you.

Below is a list of some possible meditation goals. Please rate each of them with a score of one to four, with one being irrelevant and four being the most relevant for you. For example, if your main reason for learning meditation is to combat insomnia, that would score a 4. If you are not interested in the spiritual side of meditation, that will score a 1.

1	2	3	4
Not relevant at all	Slightly relevant	Moderately relevant	Very much relevant

Goal or Benefit	1	2	3	4
1. Be less self-critical	1	2	3	4
2. Boost immunity & maintain health	1	2	3	4
3. Connect to a higher power or spirituality	1	2	3	4
4. Cultivate mindfulness & a greater level of awareness	1	2	3	4
5. Decrease anger & reactivity	1	2	3	4
6. Develop creativity, insight & intuition	1	2	3	4
7. Ease physical pain or discomfort	1	2	3	4
8. Enhance sleep & combat insomnia	1	2	3	4
9. Feel a greater sense of enjoyment in your life	1	2	3	4

10. Increase energy levels	1	2	3	4
11. Overcome addiction e.g. eating, smoking, alcohol, drugs	1	2	3	4
12. Perform better at work, school or sports	1	2	3	4
13. Prevent or manage anxiety & depression	1	2	3	4
14. Process & release emotions	1	2	3	4
15. Recover from illness, injury or surgery	1	2	3	4
16. Reduce feelings of stress & overwhelm	1	2	3	4
17. Stop overthinking & manage thoughts	1	2	3	4
18. Sustain focus & concentration	1	2	3	4

3. GETTING STARTED

"Meditation doesn't require a special set of skills. It works so well because it enhances what we already have – connection, mindfulness and compassion."

Sharon Salzberg

TIPS TO GET STARTED

The basic idea behind mindfulness meditation is simple - you sit in a comfortable position and focus on something like your breathing. When your mind wanders, you bring it back to its original task.

The goal of mindfulness meditation is not about achieving a state of bliss (although that can be a pleasant side effect). Instead, it's about training yourself to recognise when you're distracted from what you're doing and, in time, not be so easily distracted. In other words, focus on one thing at a time.

Whether you're just beginning to get into meditation or are already a regular, here are some tips for ensuring you get started and stay on the path.

 Be motivated, dedicated, and disciplined even if you don't enjoy it at first (just like eating vegetables or exercising).

 Set realistic goals for yourself, and be kind to yourself even if you become uncomfortable, restless, impatient, or emotional.

 Let go of yourself and be.

 Don't treat it as escaping from reality but embrace it more fully.

 Prepare, so you are ready to meditate and don't make excuses not to.

 Be consistent - it's better to do 10 minutes per day than one hour a week.

 Like physical exercise, 20 minutes will be more beneficial than 10, so try to work your way up to this but start with what is practical for you. 5 minutes is better than nothing.

 Keep it simple, to begin with, e.g., breath or relaxation meditation.

 Practice a meditation for at least a week before trying a different one. So you don't get overwhelmed with all the options out there.

STEPS TO GET STARTED

Although it may sound complicated, mindfulness meditation doesn't take a lot of effort. Here's how to get started:

1 PREPARATION

- Set a time you can stick to every day when you won't be distracted (at least while beginning your practice – when you become more experienced, you can meditate anywhere anytime).

- Create an inviting, dedicated space and decorate it with things that appeal to you and bring you a sense of calm and peace, e.g., candles, incense, flowers, pictures, or anything else that helps you feel relaxed and encourages the ritual. Have this set up ready to go at all times, so you don't have to spend time preparing (or procrastinating!).

2 POSITIONING

- *Cross-legged on a cushion.* If comfortable, you can sit in half or full lotus for a more stable base; with your pelvis/hips tilted forwards and higher than your knees; back upright with a neutral spine (not rigid or slouching and shoulders relaxed); hands resting on your thighs or cupped in your lap; head floating on your neck with your chin tucked in slightly.

- *Sitting on a chair.* Feet flat on the ground; sitting forward (not slouched against the back of the chair); back upright with a neutral spine (not rigid or slouching and shoulders relaxed); hands resting on your thighs or cupped in your lap; head floating on your neck with chin tucked in slightly.

- *Laying down.* Avoid it if you think it will put you to sleep (unless you are doing a relaxation meditation to get to sleep). However, if sitting is too painful or uncomfortable, using this position would be most suitable. Lying on your back (symmetrical, i.e., legs uncrossed) with your arms beside your body and palms facing upwards (to keep your shoulders relaxed); with a pillow under your thighs or head if you need the extra support for your back or neck.

3. CHOOSE YOUR ANCHOR POINT

Choose something to focus on, and each time your mind starts to wander (which it will), bring your focus back to this. You may need to do this ten times or 100 times - it doesn't matter. What matters is that you notice when your mind has wandered and gently bring it back each time. Here are some options:

- Breath - breathe in and out through the nose; observe the movement of your breath in your body, e.g. the rise and fall of your belly or chest or the air entering and leaving your nostrils. If your mind is really busy, try counting your number of breaths or naming the breath, e.g. breathing in, breathing out.

- Senses - notice the sounds around you, inside and out (without judging, just noticing), smells, touch (your clothes, air, surface you are sitting on).

- Body - scan your body, from head to your toes. Notice any tension or tightness, or sensations in any area of your body.

- Object - focus on something like a candle.

- Teacher - follow the voice in a guided meditation.

4. RELAXATION (OPTIONAL)

See if you can mentally and physically relax each part of your body each time you breathe out.

5. REST IN THE STILLNESS (OPTIONAL)

Focus on the stillness or silence, e.g. the pause between each breath or thought.

6. RECONNECT AND REFLECT

- Gently bring your awareness back into your body and the space around you - take some longer, slower breaths in through the nose and out through the mouth, wriggle your toes and fingers, stretch if you need to.

- Notice any sensations you may be feeling.

- Reflect on any insights you may have received or your intention to continue your mindful awareness throughout the rest of your day or night.

7 COMMON OBSTACLES TO MEDITATING

Overcoming your initial roadblocks in meditation practice is often part of what prevents people from getting started. The most common reasons I hear why people don't try to meditate are:

1) I don't have time for it,

2) I can't sit still,

3) My mind won't stop racing.

These are normal responses and should not be a reason to give up. Following are some possible solutions to the most common obstacles faced during meditation:

1. FEELING RESTLESS OR HAVING DIFFICULTY RELAXING:

- Try guided relaxation or Yoga Nidra meditation.

- Go for a walk or do some yoga or dancing before meditating to release some energy.

- Clench and relax each muscle group working your way from your face to your toes.

2. DROWSINESS OR FALLING ASLEEP:

- Sleepiness is fine if you are doing meditation at night with the intention of having a restful sleep.

- At any other time, try meditating in a location other than your bedroom (as your brain tends to associate this room with sleep).

- Try a sitting posture rather than lying down.

- Do some stretches or go for a walk before meditating.

- Avoid eating and drinking before meditating.

- Ensure you are getting enough sleep at night.

3. EMOTIONAL RESPONSES:

- It is common for emotions and thoughts to arise when sitting for long periods without the distractions of keeping busy.

- Crying, laughing, and farting are signs of releasing tension and will usually clear as you continue.

- Be gentle and kind to yourself until it does, and if it becomes too intense, you may wish to stop and continue later when you have processed or released the emotion.

- If persistent thoughts or emotions affect your ability to enjoy everyday life or function correctly, please seek professional counselling services.

4. DISENGAGEMENT AKA DRIFTING OFF:

- Mindfulness meditation is a means to embrace and accept life rather than trying to escape reality.

- It is normal to feel sensations of "drifting off" sometimes but essential to remain aware.

- If you are feeling dizzy, lightheaded, or disorientated, try to focus on your breathing and where you can feel the breath in your body, e.g., nostrils, chest, belly.

5. HYPERVENTILATION OR HYPOVENTILATION:

- Changes in your breathing pattern can result in decreased or increased levels of Co_2, which can cause dizziness and anxiety.

- Breathe in and out through your nostrils at your own natural pace and rhythm. If you find this challenging try breathing in through the nose and out through the mouth as though you are holding a straw between your lips.

- Do not try to hold your breath or breathe too deeply.

- Symptoms should pass, but if not, try a physical activity like walking and seek medical advice if they persist.

6. NEGATIVE ASSOCIATIONS WITH MEDITATION:

- Feeling guilty at taking this time out for yourself or being perceived as spending time doing nothing can hinder your progress.

- Remind yourself that self-care is vital for physical and mental wellbeing and conducive to harmonious relationships.

- If you do not look after yourself, it will hamper your care for others and even your performance at work, home or sport.

- Meditation can help you be more productive as it brings greater focus and clarity.

- Just like physical exercise, the key to maximising the benefits of meditation is consistency, and the longer you meditate, the greater the benefits be.

7. PHYSICAL DISCOMFORT DURING MEDITATION:

- A little bit of discomfort is okay to keep you awake and aware, but too much pain will distract you from your meditation practice and its benefits.

- Massage, rub or scratch the area. If need be, stretch and mindfully move your body into a more comfortable position.

If you're looking for a simple but effective way to boost your health and wellbeing, mindfulness meditation may be something that changes your life and is worth the obstacles!

From improving your physical and mental wellbeing to reducing stress and anxiety, there are countless benefits of taking time each day just for yourself.

By focussing on what you can control in your life and removing your self-imposed limitations, you can achieve anything you set out to do in a more effortless and less stressful manner.

SETTING UP YOUR PRACTICE

Please take a few minutes to complete the following questions to help you get started.

What benefits of meditation interest you the most?

How could you use meditation in your life?

Where could you set up a meditation space in your home, what posture would suit you best and do you need any equipment?

How long do you think you could dedicate to meditating each day and at what time?

What obstacles or challenges (if any) have you encountered when beginning to meditate?

4. BREATHING TECHNIQUES

"Meditation is the journey from sound to silence, from movement to stillness, from a limited identity to unlimited space."

Shri Ravi Shankar

BREATHING INSIGHTS

Each day, we take approximately 17,000 breaths. With every breath in, we feed oxygen to the cells all over our bodies. With each breath out, we remove toxins from the body. While breathing is something we all naturally do, how we interact with it can impact our stress, anxiety and thought processes.

Certain things impact our breathing.

For example, certain smells can invoke emotions and memories as the olfactory cortex sends signals to the amygdala (emotions) and hippocampus (memories). By focussing on our breathing during these times, we can take our attention away from distracting thoughts and emotions that may overwhelm us.

When people feel stressed, worried or fearful, our breathing tends to be shallow, quick and through the mouth rather than the nose. Breathing nasally, slowly and fully brings us back into our bodies and to the present moment.

Mindful breathing grounds and anchors us, which can lead the body into a state of relaxation and recovery.

Following the rhythm of your breath and noticing its movement in your body is one of the simplest and most effective meditation techniques to learn.

DIAPHRAGMATIC BREATHING

When you practise breathing in through the nose (i.e. nasally), on each breath in the lungs expand, pushing the diaphragm down and the belly out. This movement is why diaphragmatic breathing is also known as belly breathing.

The movement of the diaphragm massages the vagus nerve, a cranial nerve that runs from your brain to your colon. As it's massaged, it sends a message to your brain to tell it to calm down. Breathing in through the nose also lowers your heart rate making this an effective exercise when feeling anxious or overwhelmed. The additional benefits of nasal breathing include:

- More efficient oxygenation - as you are engaging the bottom part of the lungs where about two-thirds of the gas exchange occurs.

- Muscle relaxation - as you are not using your neck and shoulders to breathe, these areas have less tension.

- Reduced heart rate - rebalances the autonomic nervous system (from sympathetic, i.e. fight or flight to parasympathetic, i.e. calm and relaxation).

- Assisted lymphatic drainage and digestion - as the abdominal muscles are gently massaged.

- Improved posture and core strength.

ANCHOR POINTS

There are three parts of your body where you may notice a movement or sensation during each breath when breathing nasally:

NOSTRILS - the feel of the air flowing in and out (you may notice it's cool as you breathe in and warm as you breathe out).

CHEST - gently rises with each in-breath and lowers with each out-breath (not enough to make your shoulders move).

BELLY - expanding like a balloon on the in-breath and deflating on the out-breath.

One of these sensations will be stronger for you than the other two. Choose this as your anchor point to focus on when practising mindful breathing.

When your mind starts to wander during meditation, use your anchor point to draw your attention back to your breathing.

You could also use your anchor point to bring your attention back to any task you are doing at home or work.

BREATHING EXERCISES

Belly Breathing

Practising this breathing exercise can help:

- Reduce anxiety
- Manage stressful situations
- Bring on restful sleep
- Increase focus and clarity

SCAN TO LISTEN

SCAN TO WATCH

Lay on your back and keep your body in a symmetrical position with your legs out straight. You can also do this sitting on a chair with your feet flat on the floor, back upright and shoulders relaxed.

Place one hand on your chest and the other one on your belly.

Relax the muscles in your jaw, forehead and around your eyes as you close them.

Take three breaths in through your nose and out through your mouth, allowing your body to settle.

Begin breathing in and out through your nostrils, at your own pace, finding your natural rhythm.

Notice the sensation of the air at the base of your nostrils as you breathe in and out.

Notice the movement of the hand on your chest rising and falling as your chest expands on the in-breath and contracts on the out-breath.

Notice the movement of the hand on your belly rising and falling as your belly expands on the in-breath and contracts on the out-breath.

Choose the strongest sensation to be your anchor point, i.e. your nostrils, chest or belly.

When your mind begins to wander, gently bring your attention back to your breathing by focussing on your ancho point.

Counting or Naming the Breath

Counting or naming the breath can be an easy technique for beginners or people with hectic minds to focus their attention, distract their thoughts and get into a rhythm.

It's okay to begin meditation by counting the breath initially to focus and get settled, but then I recommend letting go of counting, so you are just observing the breath rather than concentrating too much.

Exercises:

- Counting each breath cycle up to 10 breaths.

- Counting the duration of the breath in each breath cycle, e.g. counting 1,1,1,1 on the in the breath then 1,1,1,1 on the out breath.

- Counting the duration of the breath for a count of 4, e.g. counting 1,2,3,4 on the in breath then 1,2,3,4 on the out breath (you can count to 3 or 6 if your breath is shorter or longer - match the count to your natural breath).

- Counting and naming the breath, e.g. IN 2,3,4 then OUT 2,3,4.

- Repeating the mantra "I am breathing in", "I am breathing out".

- Naming the type of breath, e.g. short, shallow, long, deep.

> If you are finding it difficult to keep track of which number breath you are on, use your fingers (mudras), e.g. left thumb up for 1, touch the tip of your thumb and first finger for 2, thumb and middle finger for 3, thumb and fourth finger is 4 then thumb and pinkie together is 5. Then start on your right hand to count from 6 to 10.

Square Breathing

Square breathing (also known as box breathing) involves taking long even breaths and pauses.

This can help reduce stress and anxiety and increase focus and clarity.

Watch the gif on my website (from destressmonday.org) - follow the movement of the ball around the square and breath with the instructions (inhale, hold, exhale, hold).

Breathe in and trace one side whilst counting to 4, hold your breath and trace the next side whilst counting to 4, breathe out and trace the third side whilst counting to 4, hold your breath and trace the fourth side whilst counting to 4.

Repeat 10 times or for a minute.

If you find it difficult to hold your breath, breathe in through your nose then out through the mouth, holding your lips as if they were around a straw.

SCAN TO WATCH

CHOOSE YOUR ANCHOR

What is your breath anchor point (nostrils, chest or belly)?

How did you feel after practising belly breathing?

Which counting the breath technique did you find the easiest or most effective?

Which naming the breath technique did you find the most effective?

Listen to the Breath Meditation (scan the QR code below) and make notes on how you felt afterwards. Were you able to bring your attention back to your breathing when your mind wandered?

5. BODY RELAXATION

"A meditation practice, deepened in silence, yields an intimacy with oneself, and over time a greater intimacy with others, and with all of life."

Beth Roth

ABOUT THE MUSCLES

We have over 600 muscles in the body. The smallest muscle is in the ear, and the strongest is in the jaw.

Muscles are made up of fibres that can shorten or lengthen. They are long and flat when relaxed and bunched up, and tight when tensed. Think of the biceps when they are flexed as an example of this.

The shoulders and jaw are two common places where we hold tension in our bodies, hence why they may feel tight when we are stressed.

> "Pain is an unpleasant sensory and emotional experience associated with, or resembling that associated with, actual or potential tissue damage."
>
> (The International Association for the Study of Pain)

ABOUT MUSCLE TENSION

When our nervous systems are stressed, the blood flow to the muscles can become reduced, causing tension.

Muscle tension is the body's defence against injury and pain, and they release tension when short term stress passes. However, with chronic or long term stress, the muscles in the body are in a constant state of tension.

Increased stress hormones, such as adrenaline and cortisol, can take a toll on the body physically as they increase things like heart rate and blood pressure. Fear, worry, and anxiety can contribute to muscle pain and tightness. Low-grade chronic stress not only leads to muscle tension but can also lead to high blood pressure.

Acute pain is short-term pain resulting from an injury or tissue damage and is usually gone when the injury heals. Chronic pain is ongoing, felt every day of the week, and can cause emotional and mental stress, especially if it prevents a person from working, exercising, socialising, sleeping, and enjoying life. Living with chronic or acute pain can be physically and emotionally demanding, making everyday activities challenging, sometimes even excruciating.

One in 5 Australians aged 45 and over live with persistent, ongoing pain.

The natural human reaction to pain is to want to push it away, hope for it to end and resist the sensation as much as possible. It's this resistance that can often exacerbate our pain or discomfort. Rather than ignoring or blocking the pain, focussing your awareness on it by doing something like a body scan can reduce the sensation.

Practising techniques such as meditation can:

- Teach you to adopt a curious mind to explore and investigate the pain.

- Change your perception and experience of pain by bringing a detached awareness to the sensation.

- Release endorphins, the body's natural pain killer.

- Relax the muscles that may be tense due to sensations of pain.

THE RELAXATION RESPONSE

Stress can present as a physical symptom in the body, such as fast and shallow breathing, increased heart rate, and sweaty palms.

By bringing our attention to these sensations in the body and recognising we are in a state of anxiety or stress, we can apply relaxation techniques to reduce and manage it.

Focussing on something like the muscle groups gets us out of the thoughts in our head and into our bodies and the present moment.

When we use tools like meditation to practise being in our bodies, sitting in stillness and quieting our minds (by giving it something else to focus on), we cultivate the Relaxation Response.

Practising relaxation exercises such as belly breathing, body scans and meditation, invokes the Relaxation Response by releasing muscle tension and slowing your heart rate. The Relaxation Response is the optimal state for the body to heal and function efficiently and effectively.

To be relaxed is to be healthy - it does not mean you are being lazy or unproductive!

RELAXATION EXERCISES
PMR

We go about our day holding tension in our bodies without realising it. If I told you right now to drop your shoulders and create a space between the top and bottom rows of your teeth, you would more than likely be able to do both, not realising you were holding your shoulders up or clenching your jaw.

Progressive Muscle Relaxation or PMR involves tensing then relaxing a group of muscles. This practice reminds your body of the difference between feeling tense and relaxed. Using PMR at night before you go to bed can help you release physical and mental tension that may otherwise interfere with sleep.

Stand somewhere you can use something like a chair or wall for balance if you need to.

Begin by taking a slow breath in through your nose, then as you are breathing out through your mouth, release a sigh. Continue to breath in through the nose and out through the mouth.

Breathe in and tense all the muscles in your face (e.g. jaw, eyes and forehead).

As you breathe out, let them all soften.

Breathe in and raise your arms in the air with your hands clenched.

Breathe out, release your fists and lower your hands and arms.

Breathe in and tense both your arms into a bicep curl.

Breathe out and let them float back down to your sides.

Breathe in and shrug your shoulders to your ears.

As you breathe out, release them and let them drop.

Breathe in and tense your stomach muscles (as if someone is going to punch you in the guts).

Breathe out and let all those muscles soften.

Breathe in and tense your glutes.

Breathe out and let them soften.

Breathe in and raise your right leg, tensing your thigh muscles and calf muscles.

Breathe out and let them soften and lower your leg.

Breathe in and raise your left leg, tensing your thigh and calf muscles.

Breathe out and let them soften and lower your leg.

Breathe in and clench your toes (as if you are trying to grab the carpet/floor).

Breathe out and let them soften.

To finish, take another slow breath in through your nose, then as you are breathing out through your mouth, release a sigh.

SCAN TO LISTEN

SCAN TO WATCH

Body Scan

A body scan is a form of Mindfulness Meditation and focuses your attention on the body's physical sensations to relax both mentally and physically.

Body scans can be used during the day to release stress and focus attention. Body scans can be used at night to help release muscle tension to prepare for sleep. It can be challenging to relax your mind if you haven't settled your body.

This process also helps manage pain, stress and anxiety as you become aware of how your stress triggers manifest in your body, e.g. sore neck at the end of a day.

By tuning in to your body, you are bringing awareness to tension you may not have noticed so that you can release it.

Begin by taking a long, slow breath in through your nose and out through your mouth.

Then let your breathing flow at a natural pace, in and out through your nostrils.

When you're ready, close your eyes.

Bring your awareness to the muscles in your face.

On your next out-breath - release any tension you may be holding in your forehead, eyes, cheeks and jaw.

Bring your awareness to the muscles and joints in your neck and shoulders.

On your next out-breath - release any tension you are holding in these areas.

Bring your awareness to the muscles in your arms, hands and fingers.

On your next out-breath - release any tension you are holding in your arms.

Bring your awareness to the muscles and joints in your back.

On your next out-breath - release any tension you are holding in this area.

Bring your awareness to the muscles in your chest and stomach.

On your next out-breath - release any tension you are holding in these areas.

Bring your awareness to the muscles and joints in your hips, pelvis and glutes.

On your next out-breath - release any tension you are holding in this area.

Bring your awareness to the muscles in thighs, shins and calves.

On your next out-breath - release any tension you are holding in your legs.

Bring your awareness to your feet and toes.

On your next out-breath - release any tension you are holding in this area.

Pain Release

If you are feeling pain or any strong or uncomfortable sensation or emotion in one particular area of the body, rather than trying to ignore it or block it, focus your breathing on this area.

SCAN TO LISTEN

Begin by practising the belly breathing exercise.

After a minute or so of focussing on your breathing, scan through your body and notice any area of tension, tightness, pain or discomfort.

Begin describing the sensation in your mind – thinking about its:

- Shape
- Size
- Colour
- Temperature
- Density
- Texture
- Depth

Once you have a clear picture of it, begin directing your breath to it. As you breathe in, visualise the breath swirling around the outside of the sensation. As you breathe out, visualise the breath taking some of that sensation away from the outside. Practise this 3-5 times or for a minute.

Then as you breathe in, visualise the breath going to the centre of the sensation. And as you breathe out, visualise the breath drawing some of that sensation away from the centre. Practise this 3-5 times or for a minute.

If any of the sensation remains after this, you could continue to practise the breathing visualisation or just allow it to be.

You could also visualise the breath as a soothing colour such as green, blue or white when you are practising this.

This exercise has been adapted from Ian Gawler's <u>Effective Pain Management</u>

CHOOSE YOUR BODY RELAXATION TECHNIQUE

Which body relaxation technique did you find the most effective?

Describe the sensation you focussed on during the pain relief exercise:

Shape:

Size:

Colour:

Temperature:

Density:

Texture:

Depth:

Listen to the Body Scan Relaxation Meditation - "The Beach" (scan the QR code below with your mobile phone's camera) and make notes on how you felt afterwards.

RELAXATION MEDITATION

6. MANAGING THOUGHTS

> "Within you there is a stillness and sanctuary you can retreat to at any time and be yourself."
>
> Hermann Hesse

THE THINKING MIND

We have around 50,000 to 80,000 thoughts per day.

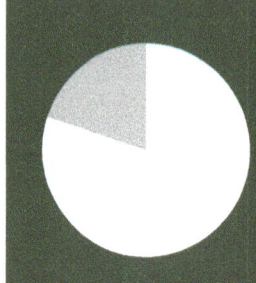

Around 80% of those are the same as the ones we had yesterday.

It is estimated that we spend more than 40% of our time lost in thought - that's almost half our waking hours!

Our brains use 25% of the body's energy – no wonder overthinking can be so physically exhausting!

Thinking about the past can cause depression.

Worrying about the future can cause anxiety.

Negative and repetitive thoughts, excessive thinking and rumination are habits that can lead people down a path of anxiety and depression, especially thinking about the past or worrying about the future.

When we become attached to a thought and constantly repeat it, consciously or unconsciously, it can become harmful.

It is okay to reflect, plan and reminisce, as long as you feel good about whatever you are planning or reflecting or reminiscing about.

BRINGING AWARENESS TO YOUR THOUGHTS

The good news is - even though your thoughts may sound challenging, you don't need to fear them!

By practising mindfulness we can bring AWARENESS to:

- The natural occurrence of overthinking - we all do it.

- Patterns and themes - you can consider jotting down your negative thoughts over a week and see if there's a pattern.

- The obsessive nature of the mind as it wants to occupy itself with thoughts.

- Triggers - either physical or emotional.

- The presence of an inner critic - the negative narrative we tell ourselves.

- Being trapped in the past or the future - are you going to allow the thinking mind to steal your present moment?

- The stories we tell ourselves and the catastrophising - this is what causes the suffering.

- The relationship between thoughts and emotions and where you feel them in your body.

- YOU HAVE A CHOICE - how do you want to engage your thinking mind?

It's about changing your habits as you become more aware of how you react to your thoughts so they no longer control you. The more you practise being mindful of your thoughts, the less they will control, distract and influence you.

9 TECHNIQUES FOR MANAGING THOUGHTS

We have the power to train our minds with a variety of techniques and interventions.

 ## 1. LABELLING

Label the thought, e.g. worrying, daydreaming, ruminating, regretting, resisting. This brings your awareness and curiosity to it and helps you see it from a different perspective. It also brings you into the present rather than being taken away by the thought. Giving your inner critic a name is also a great way to non-identity with the thoughts, i.e. they aren't you.

 ## 2. PAUSING OR PARKING

Park the thought to deal with later so it's not distracting you from the present and what you are doing right now.

3. NOTICE THE PHYSICAL SENSATIONS

Notice the physical sensations (e.g. sweaty palms, racing heart, butterflies, tightness, nausea) and how you are feeling (e.g. angry, hurt). This helps identify your triggers and provide you with a choice on how to react and what to think.

 ## 4. RESIST THE URGE TO TELL OTHERS THE STORY

Resist the urge to analyse a thought you have become attached to with a friend or family member who may sympathise with you. This only reinforces the story you are telling yourself, keeping the thoughts front and centre in your mind and retriggering the emotion the comes with them.

 ## 5. REPLACE THE THOUGHT WITH A MANTRA OR AFFIRMATION

When you notice you are ruminating, try replacing the thought with a mantra, e.g. "I am letting go of that thought" or "I choose peace." Repeating this will train your brain to redirect your mind automatically when you start to get lost in that thought again.

6. PRACTISE NON JUDGEMENT AND SELF COMPASSION

Rather than labelling the thought or experience as good or bad, try just telling yourself this is okay and "I am okay."

7. THANK THE THINKING MIND

This overrides the negative bias of the thinking mind. Imagine if you were having an argument with someone and you just stopped and said "thank you".

8. TELL THE THOUGHT OR THE INNER CRITIC TO F OFF

You are in control!

9. JOURNALING OR WRITING

This is a good technique to get the thoughts out of your head, especially if you are trying to sleep at night. You could free write what you are thinking about, create a to-do list or write a letter to someone.

Choose 3 intervention techniques to try and note which one you found the most effective.

Listen to the Letting go of Thoughts Meditation - "The Mountain" (scan the QR code opposite with your mobile phone's camera) and make notes on how you felt afterwards.

If you are having persistent thoughts that are affecting your mental, physical and emotional wellbeing or day to day ability to function or enjoy life then please seek the services of a therapist or mental health professional.

THOUGHTS MEDITATION

CONTEMPLATION EXERCISES

Thought Cloud Exercise

SCAN TO LISTEN

Sit on a chair with your feet flat on the floor, back upright and shoulders relaxed.

Let the muscles across your forehead, around your eyes and in your jaw relax.

Rest your hands on your thighs or cupped in your lap.

Take a long, slow breath in through your nose and out through your mouth, letting your body settle, and your eyes close.

Allow your breathing to flow at its natural pace, in and out through the nose, noticing the feel of the air as it enters and leaves your nostrils.

Notice the feel of your chest and belly as they rise and fall or expand and relax with each breath.

Begin visualising your mind is like a blue sky and allow your thoughts to float into your awareness like clouds. Notice how many they are and how they appear. Do they appear and disappear? Do they flow in from both sides? Do they come from one side and move across to the other side?

Bring your attention to the blue sky between the clouds and on your next out-breath, picture the clouds being pushed to the sides so there is just an expanse of blue stillness at the centre.

Allow your thought clouds to drift into your awareness again - are there as many?

On your next out-breath picture the clouds being pushed to the sides again and rest in the stillness.

Repeat this once more, noticing if the thoughts are getting less and less or appearing slower.

When you're ready open your eyes and bring your awareness back to the space around you.

Were you able to picture your thoughts like clouds and push them out of your awareness?

Thought Train Exercise

Sit on a chair with your feet flat on the floor, back upright and shoulders relaxed.

Let the muscles across your forehead, around your eyes and in your jaw relax.

Rest your hands on your thighs or cupped in your lap.

Take a long, slow breath in through your nose and out through your mouth, letting your body settle, and your eyes close.

Allow your breathing to flow at its natural pace, in and out through the nose, noticing the feel of the air as it enters and leaves your nostrils.

Notice the feel of your chest and belly as they rise and fall or expand and relax with each breath.

Visualise you are standing on a train station platform, watching your thoughts go by like trains. How fast do they come? Do they come in one steady continous stream like a high-speed train? Or do they appear like the carriages of a freight train with a thought, a pause or gap, then another thought?

Let the thoughts move on so you are standing in silence on the platform waiting for the next train.

Let the next train of thoughts come - see if you can make them stop then start again. See if you can make them go faster or slower. See if you can increase the gap between them.

Let the thoughts move on again leaving you resting in the stillness for a few breaths.

Slowly open your eyes and bring your awareness back to the space around you.

Are your thoughts in one continuous flow like a speed train or are there pauses between your thoughts like the carriages?

Starfish Meditation

Sit on a chair with your feet flat on the floor, back upright and shoulders relaxed.

Let the muscles across your forehead, around your eyes and in your jaw relax.

Rest your hands on your thighs with your palms facing upwards.

Take a long, slow breath in through your nose and out through your mouth, letting your body settle.

Allow your breathing to flow at its natural pace, in and out through the nose, noticing the feel of the air as it enters and leaves your nostrils.

Notice the feel of your chest and belly as they rise and fall or expand and relax with each breath.

Continuing to pay attention to your breathing, bring your left hand up in front of your face (palm facing towards you) and fingers apart (like a starfish).

With the index finger on your right hand, begin tracing around your left fingers, starting at the base of your thumb.

Breathe in and trace your right fingertip up the outside of your left thumb.

Breathe out and trace your right fingertip down the inside of your left thumb.

Do this around each finger of your left hand nice and slowly, taking one breath for each finger.

When you have finished the left hand, hold your right hand in front of your face and begin tracing with your left index finger, starting with the pinkie.

Breathe in and trace your left fingertip up the outside of your right pinkie.

Breathe out and trace your left fingertip down the inside of your right pinkie.

Do this with each finger on your right hand nice and slowly, taking one breath for each finger.

When finished tracing your right hand, place your palms face down on your thighs.

Take another nice slow breath in through your nose and out through your mouth.

Notice how the background behind your hand goes out of focus - you can move your thoughts to the background of your awareness in a similar way.

SCAN TO LISTEN

SCAN TO WATCH

7. RELEASING EMOTIONS

> "When we 'take the one seat' on our meditation cushion, we become our own monastery. We create the compassionate space that allows for the airing of all things – sorrows, loneliness, shame, desire, regret, frustration, happiness."
>
> Jack Kornfield

THE SCIENCE OF EMOTIONS

Emotions are energy in motion, moving through the body, that needs to be felt and released as needed.

Feelings are what's happening whilst the energy of an emotion is flowing, i.e. the physiological sensation of the emotion. For example, you may feel constriction or heaviness in the chest when sad, tightness in the jaw or hands when angry, and light and expansive when happy or joyful.

While emotions may feel draining at times, they are necessary. One of the most basic examples is that we need to feel fear to prevent us from doing dangerous things. We need to feel happiness to be able to enjoy life. The more you resist and judge an emotion, the more intense and unpleasant it can become, causing and creating emotional phobia. That's why it is better to accept, release or integrate emotions, which can help transform them into personal growth and resilience.

More often than not, the story that we tell ourselves is worse than the actual emotion we initially felt. This repetition causes us to ruminate about it even more. We need to be willing to stop the blame, self-pity and resentment and feel the anger, fear, sadness, denial, loss, sorrow, or grief.

Both positive and negative emotions can coexist. It's not a matter of one or the other, and they do not need to make sense or follow a logical pattern - no matter how much we wish them to.

NEUROSCIENCE OF EMOTIONAL ENERGY

Our emotional brain responds faster to events than our analytical brain. It is also connected to every area of the brain, whereas our analytical brain is not. That is why feelings of stress, worry, fear, or anger take priority over feelings of happiness and peace.

The emotional brain influences all decision making, thought processes, memories, and present experiences. Therefore, understanding, dealing with, and effectively using your emotional energy is vital to your happiness levels. The sensations you feel in your body hold the key to bringing awareness to behaviour patterns - transforming stress and generating lasting happiness.

Practising mindfulness and meditation can help process and release emotions stuck in the body. It also helps us become aware of where we feel emotions in our body so we can start to recognise them as soon as they are triggered, rather than become overwhelmed by them.

EMOTIONS IN THE BODY

We tend to feel emotions in the body as follows:

 FEAR can be felt in the whole upper body.

 ANXIETY may be felt in the chest and stomach.

 ANGER is quite often displayed in the face, chest and arms.

 LOVE is felt in the upper body.

 HAPPINESS is felt in the whole body.

Fear, resentment, tension result in the contraction of muscles and energy.

Happiness, joy, calm result in the expansion of muscles and energy.

Emotions can make us feel physically uncomfortable. For example, a pounding heart, tightness in our chest, feeling sick in the tummy. These emotions can lead to an array of physical sensations or feelings. Emotional exhaustion can make your body feel sore, weak and tired.

However, resisting these emotions isn't the solution as that can cause excessive thinking, shallow breathing and muscle tension, which can all contribute to disease and illness.

Taking note of repeated patterns of thoughts, feelings, or physical pain may highlight a part of you asking for acceptance.

WORKING WITH EMOTIONS IN MEDITATION

Like a broken bone, our hearts can grow stronger when they heal. As we heal through meditation, our hearts break open to feel fully.

One meditation myth is that meditation is used to block or repress emotions or thoughts.

Sitting still for long periods can bring up strong thoughts, feelings and emotions, as you are not distracted by "doing" and being busy.

By sitting in relaxation with an open heart, we can bring awareness to our feelings, allowing them to unfold as needed.

This practice is quite the opposite of blocking and repressing emotions.

Here are some ways in which you can work with emotions in meditation:

1. Focus on something like your breathing (i.e. mindfulness meditation) to lessen the intensity of the emotion.

2. Sit and be aware of what physical sensations arise, accepting them with self-compassion and just allowing them to be rather than trying to fix them.

3. Avoid judging your emotions or getting connected to your thoughts about them, e.g., the story that came with them.

4. Naming your emotions in the third person can help lessen the emphasis, e.g. there is anger in the belly, sadness in the chest, rather than using "I am angry" or "I am sad", which can emphasise the feeling more.

5. After you have recognised and named the emotion, sit with it and allow it without trying to fix or analyse it (see the R.A.I.N exercise on page 64.)

6. Cry if you need to, or go for a walk to allow the energy to shift and release - it is much easier to still your mind once any feelings have been given the attention they need.

7. Try moving up a few spots on the scale of emotions rather than trying to get from feeling something like grief to something like joy in one sitting. Refer to the Scale of Emotions (from Abraham Hicks) on the next page to see the different levels, e.g. try going from worry to boredom.

Listen to the Releasing Emotions Meditation - "The Waterfall" (scan the QR code below with your mobile phone's camera) and make notes on how you felt afterwards.

EMOTIONS MEDITATION

Moving up the Scale of Emotions
(Abraham Hicks Scale of Emotions)

Joy/Appreciation/Empowered/Freedom/Love
Passion
Enthusiasm/Eagerness/Happiness
Positive Expectations/Belief/Optimism
Hopefulness
Contentment
Boredom
Pessimism
Frustration/Irritation/Impatience
Overwhelment
Disappointment
Doubt
Worry
Blame
Discouragement
Anger/Revenge
Hatred/Rage
Jealousy
Insecurity/Guilt/Unworthiness
Fear/Grief/Despair/Powerlessness

Move up the emotional Scale →

If you find that a feeling stays present for any length of time or you are feeling overwhelmed with emotion, it is important to seek additional support via counselling.

RELEASING EXERCISES
Colour Breath Exercise

SCAN TO LISTEN

Sit on a chair with your feet flat on the floor, back upright and shoulders relaxed.

Let the muscles across your forehead, around your eyes and in your jaw relax.

Rest your hands on your thighs or cupped in your lap.

Take a long, slow breath in through your nose and out through your mouth, letting your body settle and your eyes to close.

Allow your breathing to flow at its natural pace, in and out through the nose.

Bring your attention to your throat, noticing the feel of the air as it flows up and down. Notice any other sensations that may be present, e.g. constriction, tightness, scratchiness.

Begin visualising that with each in-breath you breathe in a cool blue colour, the colour filling your throat with each breath.

On each out-breath, visualise you are releasing any of those unwanted sensations which may be trapped emotional energy in your throat.

Bring your attention to your chest, noticing how it rises and falls gently with each breath. Notice any other sensations that may be present, e.g. constriction, tightness, heaviness.

Begin visualising that with each in-breath you breathe in a cool green colour, the colour filling your chest with each breath.

On each out-breath, visualise you are releasing any of those unwanted sensations which may be trapped emotional energy in your chest.

Bring your attention to your belly, noticing how it gently expands and relaxes with each breath. Notice any other sensations that may be present, e.g. bubbling, cramping, nausea.

Begin visualising that with each in-breath you breathe in a warm red, orange or yellow colour, the colour filling your belly with each breath.

On each out-breath, visualise you are releasing any of those unwanted sensations which may be trapped emotional energy in your belly.

Mantras

Scientific studies have shown that repetition of a single word can lower blood pressure, slow the heart rate and calm brainwave activity. Repeating words and thought patterns tricks the brain into thinking in these new ways. Affirmations are a statement of intent, chosen and spoken consciously, to establish a subconscious belief or desire. Using mantras and affirmations can:

- Promote relaxation and healing.
- Develop confidence and self-esteem.
- Override negative thoughts.
- Be used as a tool to create your desired reality.

Some of my favourites when I start getting hijacked by my thoughts and the emotions they bring are:

- "I choose peace over this" (Gabby Bernstein).
- "May I be happy, may I be healthy, may I be safe, may I live with ease (Sharon Salzberg).
- "I'm sorry, please forgive me, thank you, I love you." (Ho'oponopono).

Something as simple as "I am okay" is also good.

Mudras

Mudra means "seal" or "closure" in Sanskrit (the original language of Hinduism and Buddhism). They are hand gestures that channel your body's energy flow, and there are more than 100 different mudras with different benefits. Mudras are done in conjunction with mindful breathing to enhance the flow of energy or life force known as Prana.

Different areas of the hands and fingers are connected with different areas of the body and brain:

- Thumb & index finger - concentration, knowledge, insight.
- Thumb & middle finger - intuition, emotions, thoughts.
- Thumb & ring finger - metabolism, digestion, immunity.
- Thumb & pinkie - clarity, communication.

Mudra Exercise

Sit on a chair with your feet flat on the floor, back upright and shoulders relaxed.

Let the muscles across your forehead, around your eyes and in your jaw relax.

Rest your hands on your thighs with your palms facing upwards.

Take a long, slow breath in through your nose and out through your mouth, letting your body settle.

Allow your breathing to flow at its natural pace, in and out through the nose, noticing the feel of the air as it enters and leaves your nostrils.

Notice the feel of your chest and belly as they rise and fall or expand and relax with each breath.

Take a breath in and bring your thumbs and your index fingertips together, and on the out-breath say the words "I am confident and curious."

Take a breath in and bring your thumbs and your middle fingertips together, and on the out-breath say the words "I am calm and content."

Take a breath in and bring your thumbs and your ring fingertips together, and on the out-breath say the words "I am comfortable and complete."

Take a breath in and bring your thumbs and your pinkie fingertips together, and on the out-breath say the words "I am clear and kind."

Adapt or change the words to what resonates with you.

SCAN TO LISTEN

SCAN TO WATCH

R.A.I.N. Practice

This acronym is a tool for practising mindfulness and self-compassion when experiencing particularly strong or lingering emotions. I have adapted this from Tara Brach and you can go to her website for more R.A.I.N. meditations and downloads.

 **RECOGNISE**

- Acknowledge the emotion.
- Label the emotion (e.g. worry, anger, sadness, fear).
- Notice where you are feeling it in your body.

 **ALLOW**

- Accept the emotion if possible but don't force it (e.g. grief).
- If you can't accept it right now then just allow it and hold space for it, don't try to fix it.
- Avoid resisting the emotion.

 **INVESTIGATE**

- Be present with the emotion and the story behind it.
- Be curious as to why you are feeling this way.
- Connect with your intuition rather than trying to logically analyse this sensation.

 **NON IDENTIFY**

- Know that you are not your emotion (e.g. being angry doesn't make you an angry person).
- Nurture yourself until the emotion passes or changes (moving up the emotional scale with self-compassion).
- It doesn't need to be resisted as it flows through your body - it will pass.

8. WHAT NEXT

> "There is a life force within your soul, seek that life. There is a gem in the mountain of your body, seek that mine. Oh traveller, if you are in search of that, don't seek outside, look inside yourself and seek that."
>
> Rumi

28 DAY MEDITATION PLAN

This tool it to assist you with establishing a meditation practice. Maintaining this routine for 28 days will help it become a habit. Some tips to help you:

1. Get clear on your goals but don't become fixated by them.
2. Be realistic about your level of commitment and the time you have.
3. Establish a regular time and place.
4. Understand the technique/s you are going to use.
5. Have your playlist of meditations you can access easily.

(refer to the Getting Started chapter for more tips)

Before you start your plan be clear on:

WHAT practice or technique you are going to do – such as mindful breathing or a body scan:

WHEN you are going to do it – schedule the time of the day and day of the week into your calendar:

WHERE you are going to do it - a room or space in a room you have set aside or an outdoor area:

HOW you are going to achieve this – what actions you may need to take like asking your family for privacy, setting an alarm each day, having your meditation area prepared and ready:

	Day/Date	Duration	Technique	Observations
01				
02				
03				
04				
05				
06				
07				
08				
09				
10				
11				
12				
13				
14				

	Day/Date	Duration	Technique	Observations
15				
16				
17				
18				
19				
20				
21				
22				
23				
24				
25				
26				
27				
28				

CONTINUE YOUR JOURNEY

There are many ways you can continue on your journey towards creating a calm mind and body and further your understanding of mindfulness meditation. Here are some of my options:

Enrol in one of my **Online Meditation courses**.

Register for my five-week **Mindfulness Meditation for Beginners** online group program – check my websites and facebook page for dates.

Book a **Mindfulness Coaching Session** with me – options include face to face or online, individual or small groups.

Join the **4 Week Introduction to Mindfulness and Meditation program** I facilitate through Mindfulness Works Australia – check my website and facebook page for dates and locations.

Sign up for one of my 4 day **Cultivating a Calm Mind Retreats** – check my websites and Facebook page for dates and locations.

Sign up for my Bush to Beach **Campervanning Meditation Retreat** – check my websites and Facebook page for dates.

If you have any questions or would like to talk through the next best steps for you, please contact me at michelle@cultivatingacalmmind.com

Together we can establish a mindfulness meditation practice best suited for your lifestyle.

For more information, tips, tools, resources, and meditations, please follow me at:

- www.cultivatingacalmmind.com
- www.meditationsunshinecoast.com.au
- www.facebook.com/meditationsunshinecoast
- www.instagram.com/meditationsunshinecoast
- www.insighttimer.com/m3d1t8

9. ABOUT M.E.
(MICHELLE ECKLES)

"

It is in the stillness that we find peace, acceptance, compassion, clarity, wisdom and ourselves.

Michelle Eckles

Like most people, I began learning meditation during a challenging period in my life. I was separated, running a business that was no longer financially viable, selling a home I loved, and driving a very unreliable car, whilst being a single parent to two kids.

I was utterly overwhelmed, taking strong medication for chronic back pain, and drinking myself to sleep every night. I needed something not just to help reduce the feelings of anxiety and overwhelm (without antidepressants) but to also prevent me from getting to that state in the first place.

When I tried to meditate, I couldn't sit still for more than 5 minutes or count to 10 breaths! I struggled to learn through an app or on my own, so I began researching teachers and studying mindfulness and meditation.

As a result, I completed various education and qualifications, including Mindfulness Meditation Teacher Training, an Advanced Certificate in Guiding and Teaching Meditation, Corporate Mindfulness, and Mindfulness for Wellbeing & Peak Performance.

Realising how beneficial these tools would be for kids, I also completed Connected Kids, Meditation Capsules, Inspired Kids Yoga, Calm Kids Coaching, Meditation for Parents and Children, Sensory Detective (Autism Spectrum) and Youth Psychology and Counselling.

Since 2017, I have been teaching mindfulness and meditation to adults, teens, and kids.

During that time, I moved home again, shut down my party business, opened and closed a meditation studio, travelled the world managing events for high-profile speakers (including Brene Brown, Simon Sinek and the Obamas), and lost that job due to you know what.

I may not have done all these things with complete grace, but I credit my ability to transition through all of it without falling apart or contemplating drowning in a bottle to my meditation practice.

It has not only made me feel calmer, more peaceful, and resilient, but it has also increased my clarity, creativity, productivity, and focus.

As my mum likes to say - I am living proof that this shit works!

CULTIVATING A CALM MIND

Mindfulness and meditation education is now my full-time focus and passion.

I enjoy bringing the practical applications of mindfulness and meditation to the home and the workplace by educating others and demonstrating the profound mental, emotional and physical benefits it can have in your day-to-day life.

As well as offering workshops, programs, and online courses, I facilitate programs for Mindfulness Works Australia, run community classes as a service provider for the council's Healthy Sunshine Coast Program, and am a certified supplier on Career Money Life.

I am a member of the Meditation Association of Australia and mindful.org, and a Veriditas trained and certified Labyrinth Facilitator.

WWW.CULTIVATINGACALMMIND.COM | WWW.MEDITATIONSUNSHINECOAST.COM.AU